LIBRETTO

The Pirates
of Penzance
or
The Slave Of Duty

07836 662620

© 2010 by Faber Music Ltd
First published by International Music Publications Ltd
International Music Publications Ltd is a Faber Music company
Bloomsbury House 74–77 Great Russell Street London WC1B 3DA
Printed in England by Caligraving Ltd
All rights reserved

ISBN10: 0-571-53579-8
EAN13: 978-0-571-53579-8

To buy Faber Music publications or to find out about the full range of titles available,
please contact your local music retailer or Faber Music sales enquiries:

Faber Music Ltd, Burnt Mill, Elizabeth Way, Harlow, CM20 2HX England
Tel: +44(0)1279 82 89 82   Fax: +44(0)1279 82 89 83
sales@fabermusic.com   fabermusic.com

THE PIRATES OF PENZANCE

or

The Slave of Duty

DRAMATIS PERSONAE

MAJOR-GENERAL STANLEY

THE PIRATE KING

SAMUEL (his Lieutenant)

FREDERIC (the Pirate Apprentice)

SERGEANT OF POLICE

MABEL, EDITH, KATE, ISABEL (General Stanley's Daughters)

RUTH (A Piratical Maid of all Work)

Chorus of Pirates, Police and General Stanley's Daughters

ACT I.—A Rocky Seashore on the Coast of Cornwall

ACT II.—A Ruined Chapel by Moonlight

MUSICAL NUMBERS

ACT I

ACT II

ACT 1

SCENE—*A rocky seashore on the coast of Cornwall. As the curtain rises groups of pirates are discovered—some drinking, some playing cards.* SAMUEL, *the Pirate Lieutenant, is going from one group to another, filling the cups from a flask.* FREDERIC *is seated in a despondent attitude at the back of the scene.* RUTH *kneels at his feet.*

Music No. 1.	OPENING CHORUS OF PIRATES, and SOLO (Samuel) "Pour, Oh Pour, the Pirate Sherry"
ALL	Pour, oh pour, the pirate sherry; Fill, oh fill, the pirate glass! And, to make us more than merry, Let the pirate bumper pass!
SAMUEL	For today our Pirate 'Prentice Rises from indenture freed; Strong his arm and keen his scent is, He's a Pirate now indeed!
ALL	Here's good luck to Fred'ric's ventures! Fred'ric's out of his indentures.
SAMUEL	Two-and-twenty now he's rising, And alone he's fit to fly, Which we're bent on signalizing With unusual revelry.
CHORUS **plus SAMUEL**	Here's good luck to Fred'ric's ventures! Fred'ric's out of his indentures.. Pour! oh pour, the pirate sherry, Fill, oh fill, the pirate glass! And, to make us more than merry, Let the pirate bumper pass!

(FREDERIC *rises and comes forward with* PIRATE KING, *who enters*)

KING	Yes, Frederic, from today you rank as a full-blown member of our band.
ALL	Hurrah!
FREDERIC	My friends, I thank you all, from my heart, for your kindly wishes. Would that I could repay them as they deserve!
KING	What do you mean?
FREDERIC	Today I am out of my indentures, and today I leave you for ever.
KING	But this is quite unaccountable; a keener hand at scuttling a Cunarder or cutting out a P. and O. never shipped a handspike.

FREDERIC	Yes, I have done my best for you. And why? It was my duty under my indentures, and I am the slave of duty. As a child I was ~~regularly~~ apprenticed to your band. It was through an error—no matter, the mistake was ours, not yours, and I was in honour bound by it.
SAMUEL	An error? What error?
FREDERIC	I may not tell you; it would reflect upon my well-loved Ruth.

(RUTH *rises and comes forward*)

RUTH	Nay, dear master, my mind has long been gnawed by the cankering tooth of mystery. Better have it out at once.
Music No. 2.	SONG (Ruth) "When Fred'ric was a Little Lad"

RUTH

When Fred'ric was a little lad he proved so brave and daring,
His father thought he'd 'prentice him to some career seafaring.
I was, alas! his nurs'rymaid, and so it fell to *my* lot
To take and bind the promising boy apprentice to a *pilot*;
A life not bad for a hardy lad, though surely not a high lot,
Though I'm a nurse, you might do worse, than make your boy a pilot!

I was a stupid nurs'rymaid, on breakers always steering,
And I did not catch the word aright, through being hard of hearing;
Mistaking my instructions, which within my brain did gyrate,
I took and bound this promising boy apprentice to a *Pirate*!
A sad mistake it was to make, and doom him to a vile lot,
I bound him to a Pirate-you!—Instead of to a pilot!

I soon found out, beyong all doubt, the scope of this disaster,
But I hadn't the face to return to my place, and break it to my master.
A nurs'rymaid is not afraid of what you people *call* work,
So I made up my mind to go as a kind of piratical maid-of-all-work.
And that is how you find me now, a member of your shy lot,
Which you wouldn't have found, had he been bound apprentice to a pilot

RUTH	Oh, pardon! Frederic, pardon! (*Kneels*)
FREDERIC	Rise, sweet one, I have long pardoned you.
RUTH	(*rises*) The two words were so much alike!
FREDERIC	They were. They still are, ~~though years have rolled over their heads.~~ But this afternoon my obligation ceases. Individually, I love you all with affection unspeakable, but, collectively, I look upon you with a disgust that amounts to absolute detestation. Oh! pity me, my beloved friends, for such is my sense of duty that, once out of my indentures, I shall feel myself bound to devote myself heart and soul to your extermination!
ALL	Poor lad—poor lad! (*All weep*)
KING	Well, Frederic, if you conscientiously feel that it is your duty to destroy us, we cannot blame you for acting on that conviction. Always act in

KING (**Contd.**)	accordance with the dictates of your conscience, my boy, and chance the consequences.
SAMUEL	Besides, we can offer you but little temptation to remain with us. We don't seem to make piracy pay. I'm sure I don't know why, but we don't.
FREDERIC	*I* know why, but, alas! I mustn't tell you; it wouldn't be right.
KING	Why not, my boy? It's only half-past eleven, and you are one of us until the clock strikes twelve.
SAMUEL	True, and until then you are bound to protect our interests.
ALL	Hear, hear!
FREDERIC	Well, then, it is my duty, as a pirate, to tell you that you are too tender-hearted. For instance, you make a point of never attacking a weaker party than yourselves, and when you attack a stronger party you invariably get thrashed.
KING	There is some truth in that.
FREDERIC	Then, again, you make a point of never ~~molesting~~ picking on an orphan!
SAMUEL	Of course: we are orphans ourselves, and know what it is.
FREDERIC	Yes, but it has got about, and what is the consequence? Every one we capture says he's an orphan. The last three ships we took proved to be manned entirely by orphans, and so we had to let them go. One would think that Great Britain's mercantile navy was recruited solely from her orphan ~~asylums~~ orphanage—which we know is not the case.
SAMUEL	But, hang it all! you wouldn't have us absolutely merciless?
FREDERIC	There's my difficulty; until twelve o'clock I would, after twelve I wouldn't. Was ever a man placed in so delicate a situation?
RUTH	And Ruth, your own Ruth, whom you love so well, and who has won her middle-aged way into your boyish heart, what is to become of *her*?
KING	Oh, he will take you with him. (*Hands* RUTH *to* FREDERIC)
FREDERIC	Well, Ruth, I feel some little difficulty about you. It is true that I admire you very much, but I have been constantly at sea since I was eight years old, and yours is the only woman's face I have seen during that time. I think it is a sweet face.
RUTH	It is—oh, it is!
FREDERIC	I say I *think* it is; that is my impression. But as I have never had an opportunity of comparing you with other women, it is just possible I may be mistaken.
KING	True.

FREDERIC	What a terrible thing it would be if I were to marry this innocent person, and then find out that she is, on the whole, plain!
KING	Oh, Ruth is very well, very well indeed.
SAMUEL	Yes, there are the remains of a fine woman about Ruth.
FREDERIC	Do you really think so?
SAMUEL	I do.
FREDERIC	Then I will not be so selfish as to take her from you. In justice to her, and in consideration for you, I will leave her behind. (*Hands* RUTH *to* KING)
KING	No, Frederic, this must not be. We are rough men who lead a rough life, but we are not so utterly heartless as to deprive thee of thy love. I think I am right in saying that there is not one here who would rob thee of this inestimable treasure for all the world holds dear.
ALL	(*Loudly*) Not one!
KING	No, I thought there wasn't. Keep thy love, Frederic, keep thy love. (*Hands her back to* FREDERIC)
FREDERIC	You're very good, I'm sure.
	Exit RUTH
KING	Well, it's the top of the tide, and we must be off. Farewell, Frederic. When your process of extermination begins, let our deaths be as swift and painless as you can conveniently make them.
FREDERIC	I will! By the love I have for you, I swear it! Would that you could render this extermination unnecessary by accompanying me back to civilisation!
KING	No, Frederic, it cannot be. I don't think much of our profession, but, contrasted with respectability, it is comparatively honest. No, Frederic, I shall live and die a Pirate King.
Music No. 3.	SONG (Pirate King and Chorus) "Oh, Better Far to Live and Die"
KING	Oh, better far to live and die Under the brave black flag I fly, Than play a sanctimonious part, With a pirate head and a pirate heart. Away to the cheating world go you, Where pirates all are well-to-do, But I'll be true to the song I sing, And live and die a Pirate King, For I am a Pirate King! And it is, it is a glorious thing

Play.

4

KING (Contd.)	To be a Pirate King! For I am a Pirate King!
CHORUS	You are! Hurrah for our Pirate King!
KING	And it is, it is a glorious thing To be a Pirate King!
CHORUS	It is! Hurrah for our Pirate King
ALL	Hurrah for the/our Pirate King!
KING	When I sally forth to seek my prey I help myself in a royal way; I sink a few more ships, it's true, Than a well-bred monarch ought to do! But many a king on a first-class throne, If he wants to call his crown his own, Must manage somehow to get through More dirty work than ever *I* do. For I am a Pirate King! And it is, it is a glorious thing To be a Pirate King! For I am a Pirate King!
CHORUS	You are! Hurrah for our Pirate King!
KING	And it is, it is a glorious thing To be a Pirate King!
CHORUS	It is! Hurrah for our Pirate King
ALL	Hurrah for the/our Pirate King!

Exeunt all except FREDERIC

Enter RUTH

RUTH	Oh, take me with you! I cannot live if I am left behind.
FREDERIC	Ruth, I will be quite candid with you. You are very dear to me, as you know, but I must be circumspect. You see, you are considerably older than I. A lad of twenty-one usually looks for a wife of seventeen.
RUTH	A wife of seventeen! You will find me a wife of a thousand!
FREDERIC	No, but I shall find you a wife of forty-seven, and that is quite enough. Ruth, tell me candidly, and without reserve: compared with other women—how are *you*?

RUTH	I will answer you truthfully, master—I have a slight cold, but otherwise I am quite well.
FREDERIC	I am sorry for your cold, but I was referring rather to your personal appearance. Compared with other women, are you beautiful?
RUTH	(*Bashfully*) I have been told so, dear master.
FREDERIC	Ah, but lately?
RUTH	Oh, no, years and years ago.
FREDERIC	What do you think of yourself?
RUTH	It is a delicate question to answer, but I think I am a fine woman.
FREDERIC	That is your candid opinion?
RUTH	Yes, I should be deceiving you if I told you otherwise.
FREDERIC	Thank you, Ruth, I believe you, for I am sure you would not practise on my inexperience; I wish to do the right thing, and if—I say *if*—you are really a fine woman, your age shall be no obstacle to our union! (*Chorus of Girls heard in the distance*) Hark! Surely I hear voices! Who has ventured to approach our all but inaccessible lair? Can it be Custom House? No, it does not sound like Custom House.
RUTH	(*Aside*) Confusion! It is the voices of young girls. If he should see them I am lost.
FREDERIC	(*Looking off*) By all that's marvellous, a bevy of beautiful maidens!
RUTH	(*Aside*) Lost! lost! lost!
FREDERIC	How lovely! how surpassingly lovely is the plainest of them! What grace—what delicacy—what refinement! And Ruth—Ruth told me she was beautiful!
Music No. 4.	RECITATIVE & DUET (Ruth and Frederic) "Oh, False One, You have Deceiv'd Me!"
FREDERIC	Oh, false one, you have deceiv'd me!
RUTH	I have deceiv'd you?
FREDERIC	Yes! deceiv'd me! (*Denouncing her*) You told me you were fair as gold!
RUTH	(*Wildly*) And, master, am I not so?
FREDERIC	And now I see you're plain and old!
RUTH	I'm sure I'm not a jot so.

SP

— SING

6

FREDERIC	Upon my innocence you play,
RUTH	I'm not the one to plot so.
FREDERIC	Your face is lined, your hair is grey.
RUTH	It's gradually got so.
FREDERIC	Faithless woman to deceive me, I who trusted so!
RUTH	Master, master, do not leave me, Hear me, ere you go!
FREDERIC	Faithless woman!
RUTH	Master, master,
FREDERIC	Faithless woman,
RUTH	Master, master,

FREDERIC
Faithless woman to deceive me,
I who trusted so!
Faithless woman to deceive me,
I who trusted so!

RUTH
Do not leave me, do not leave me,
Hear me ere you go!
Master, master, do not leave me,
Hear me ere you go!

RUTH	My love without reflecting, Oh, do not be rejecting! Take a maiden tender—her affection raw and green, At very highest rating, Has been accumulating Summers seventeen—summers seventeen.

RUTH
Don't, beloved master,
Crush me with disaster;
What is such a dower to the dower I have here?

FREDERIC
Yes, your former master
Saves you from disaster;
Your love would be uncomfortably
       fervid, it is clear,

My love un-a-
bating
Has been accu-
mulating
Forty-seven
year,
forty-seven year!

If, as you are stating

It's been accumulating

Forty-seven
year!

FREDERIC	Faithless woman to deceive me, I who trusted so!

RUTH
Master, master, do not leave me,
Hear me, ere you go!

FREDERIC
Faithless woman to deceive me,
I who trusted so!

(At the end he renounces her, and she goes off in despair)

7

FREDERIC (recit.) What shall I do? Before these gentle maidens
I dare not show in this alarming costume!
No, no, I must remain in close concealment
Until I can appear in decent clothing!

(Hides in cave as they enter climbing over the rocks)

Music No. 5. CHORUS OF GIRLS
"Climbing Over Rocky Mountain"

GIRLS Climbing over rocky mountain,
Skipping rivulet and fountain,
Passing where the willows quiver,
Passing where the willows quiver
By the ever-rolling river,
Swollen with the summer rain, the summer rain;
Threading long and leafy mazes
Dotted with unnumbered daisies,
Dotted, dotted with unnumbered daisies;
Scaling rough and rugged passes,
Climb the hardy little lassies,
Till the bright seashore they gain;
Scaling rough and rugged passes,
Climb the hardy little lassies,
Till the bright seashore they gain!

EDITH Let us gaily tread the measure,
Make the most of fleeting leisure;
Hail it as a true ally,
Though it perish by-and-by.

CHORUS Hail it as a true ally,
Though it perish by-and-by.

EDITH Ev'ry moment brings a treasure
Of its own especial pleasure,
Though the moments quickly die,
Greet them gaily as they fly,
Greet them gaily as they fly.

CHORUS Though the moments quickly die,
Greet them gaily as they fly.

KATE Far away from toil and care,
Revelling in fresh sea air,
Here we live and reign alone
In a world that's all our own.
Here, in this our rocky den
Far away from mortal men,
We'll be Queens, and make decrees,—
They may honour them who please.

CHORUS We'll be Queens, and make decrees,
They may honour them who please.

8

ALL	Let us gaily tread the measure, Make the most of fleeting leisure, Hail it as a true ally, Though it perish by-and-by, Hail it as a true ally, Though it perish by-and-by. Let us gaily tread the measure, Make the most of fleeting leisure, Hail it as a true ally, a true ally.
KATE	What a picturesque spot! I wonder where we are!
EDITH	And I wonder where papa is? We have left him ever so far behind.
ISABEL	Oh, he will be here presently! Remember poor papa is not as young as we are, and we came over a rather difficult country.
KATE	But how thoroughly delightful it is to be so entirely alone! Why, in all probability we are the first human beings who ever set foot on this enchanting spot.
ISABEL	Except the mermaids—it's the very place for mermaids.
KATE	Who are only human beings down to the waist!
EDITH	And who can't be said strictly to set *foot* anywhere. Tails they may, but feet they *cannot*.
KATE	But what shall we do until papa and the servants arrive with the luncheon?
EDITH	We are quite alone, and the sea is as smooth as glass. Suppose we take off our shoes and stockings and paddle?
ALL	Yes, yes! The very thing! (*They prepare to carry out the suggestion. They have all taken off one shoe, when* FREDERIC *comes forward from cave*)
Music No. 6.	RECITATIVE (Edith, Kate, Frederic and Chorus of Girls) "Stop, Ladies, Pray!"
FREDERIC	Stop, ladies, pray!
CHORUS of GIRLS (*hopping on one foot*)	A man!
FREDERIC	I had intended Not to intrude myself upon your notice In this effective but alarming costume, But under these peculiar circumstances, It is my bounden duty to inform you That your proceedings will not be unwitness'd!
EDITH	But who are you, sir? Speak! (*All hopping*)
FREDERIC	I am a Pirate!
CHORUS of GIRLS (*recoiling, hopping*)	A Pirate! Horror!

FRED – But wait!
PLAY

9

FREDERIC	Ladies, do not shun me! This evening I renounce my vile profession, And, to that end, O pure and peerless maidens! Oh, blushing buds of ever-blooming beauty! I, sore at heart, I, sore at heart, implore your kind assistance.
EDITH	How pitiful his tale!
KATE	How rare his beauty!
CHORUS	How pitiful his tale! How rare his beauty!
Music No. 7.	SONG (Frederic and Chorus of Girls) "Oh, Is There not One Maiden Breast"
FREDERIC	Oh, is there not one maiden breast Which does not feel the moral beauty Of making worldly interest Subordinate to sense of duty? Who would not give up willingly All matrimonial ambition, To rescue such an one as I From his unfortunate position! From his position, To rescue such an one as I From his unfortunate position!
CHORUS	Alas, there's not one maiden breast Which seems to feel the moral beauty Of making worldly interest Subordinate to sense of duty!
FREDERIC	Oh, is there not one maiden here Whose homely face and bad complexion Have caused all hope to disappear Of ever winning man's affection? To such an one, if such there be, I swear by Heaven's arch above you, If you will cast your eyes on me— However plain you be—I'll love you! However plain you be, If you will cast your eyes on me— However plain you be—I'll love you, I'll love you, I'll love, I'll love you!
CHORUS	Alas! there's not one maiden here Whose homely face and bad complexion Have caus'd all hope to disappear Of ever winning man's affection!
FREDERIC	(*In despair*) Not one?
CHORUS	No, no—not one!

FREDERIC	Not one?
CHORUS	No, no!

MABEL enters

MABEL	Yes, one!
CHORUS	'Tis Mabel!
MABEL	Yes, 'tis Mabel! Oh, sisters, deaf to pity's name, For shame! It's true that he has gone astray, But pray Is that a reason good and true Why you Should all be deaf to pity's name?
CHORUS	(*Aside*) The question is, had he not been A thing of beauty, Would she be sway'd by quite as keen A sense of duty?
MABEL	For shame! for shame! for shame!
Music No. 8.	SONG (Mabel and Chorus of Girls) "Poor Wand'ring One!"
MABEL	Poor wand'ring one! Tho' thou hast surely strayed, Take heart of grace, Thy steps retrace, Poor wand'ring one! Poor wand'ring one! If such poor love as mine Can help thee find True peace of mind— Why, take it, it is thine!
CHORUS	Take heart, no danger lowers; Take any heart but ours!
MABEL	Take heart, fair days will shine; Take any heart—take mine!
CHORUS	Take heart, no danger lowers! Take any heart but ours!
MABEL	Take heart, fair days will shine; Take any heart—take mine! Ah! Ah! Ah! Ah! (*Cadenza*).

MABEL (Contd.)   Poor wand'ring one!
                       Tho' thou hast surely stray'd,
                       Take heart of grace,
                       Thy steps retrace,
                       Poor wand'ring

MABEL	**CHORUS**
one!	Poor wand'ring one!
Ah, ah! Ah, ah,	
ah!	Poor wand'ring one!
Ah, ah! Ah, ah, ah!	
Fair days will	Take
shine,	heart,
Take heart! - -	Take heart!
- - - - - -	Take
Take	any
mine!	heart—
Take	but
heart - - - -	ours!
- - - - - -	Take heart!
- - - - - -	Take heart!
Take	
mine!	Take
	heart! no danger lowers;
	Take any heart but ours.
	Take
Ah! ah! - - -	
- - - - - -	heart, take heart,
- - - - - -	Take
Ah! (*Cadenza ad. lib.*)	any heart—but ours,
Take heart.	Take heart.

Exeunt MABEL *and* FREDERIC

(EDITH *beckons her sisters, who form in a semi-circle around her*)

Music No. 9.   (Edith, Kate and Chorus of Girls)
                       "What Ought We to Do?"

EDITH   What ought we to do,
                       Gentle sisters, say?
                       Propriety, we know,
                       Says we ought to stay;
                       While sympathy exclaims,
                       "Free them from your tether—
                       Play at other games—
                       Leave them here together."

KATE   Her case may, any day,
                       Be yours, my dear, or mine.
                       Let her make her hay
                       While the sun doth shine.
                       Let us compromise,

| KATE (Contd.) | (Our hearts are not of leather;)
Let us shut our eyes,
And talk about the weather. |

| CHORUS | Yes, yes, let's talk about the weather. |

| Music No. 10 | DUET (Mabel and Frederic, and Chorus of Girls)
"How Beautifully Blue the Sky" |

| GIRLS | How beautifully blue the sky,
The glass is rising very high,
Continue fine I hope it may,
And yet it rain'd but yesterday.
Tomorrow it may pour again,
(I hear the country wants some rain,)
Yet people say, I know not why,
That we shall have a warm July.
Tomorrow it may pour again,
(I hear the country wants some rain,)
Yet people say, I know not why,
That we shall have a warm July, |

Enter MABEL *and* FREDERIC

(*During* MABEL's *solo the* GIRLS *continue chatter pianissimo, but listening eagerly all the time*)

| **MABEL** | | **CHORUS**
Tomorrow it may pour again,
(I hear the country
wants some rain,) Yet people say,
I know not why,
That we shall have a warm July. |
| Did ever
maiden wake
From dream
of home-
ly duty, | | |

| MABEL | To find her daylight break
With such exceeding beauty?
Did ever maiden close
Her eyes on waking sadness,
To dream of such exceeding gladness! |

| FREDERIC | Ah, yes! ah, yes! this is exceeding gladness. |

| CHORUS | How beautiful blue the sky,
The glass is rising very high,
Continue fine I hope it may.
And yet it rain'd but yesterday.
Tomorrow it may pour again,
(I hear the country wants some rain,)
Yet people say, I know not why,
That we shall have a warm July.
Tomorrow it may pour again,
(I hear the country wants some rain,) |

CHORUS (Contd.)   Yet people say, I know not why,
That we shall have a warm July.

(During FREDERIC's *solo the* GIRLS *continue their chatter pianissimo as before, but listening intently all the time)*

FREDERIC	**CHORUS** Tomorrow it may pour again,
Did ever	(I hear the country
pirate	wants some rain)

FREDERIC   roll
His soul in guilty dreaming,
And wake to find that soul
With peace and virtue beaming!

CHORUS   How beautifully blue the sky,
The glass is rising very high;
Continue fine I hope it may,
And yet it rain'd but yesterday;
Continue fine I hope it may,
And yet it rain'd but yester-

MABEL	**FREDERIC**	**CHORUS**
Did ever maiden	Did ever pirate	day. How beautifully blue the sky, The
wake From dream	loathed, Forsake	glass is rising very
of home-	his hi-	high, Continue fine I hope it
lu duty,	deous mission,	may, And yet it rain'd but yester-
To find her day-	To find himself	day. Tomorrow it may pour a-
light break With such	betrothed to la-	gain, (I hear the country wants some
exceed-	dy of	rain,) Yet people say, I know not
ing beauty!	position!	why, That we shall
		have a warm Ju-
Ah, yes! - - -	Ah, yes! - - -	ly, Yet people say, I know not why,
- - - - - -	- - - - - -	That we shall have a
Ah,	Ah,	warm July, a
yes, Ah yes!	yes, Ah yes!	warm July.

Music No. 11.   RECITATIVE (Frederic and Chorus of Girls and Pirates)
"Stay, We Must not Lose our Senses"

FREDERIC   Stay, we must not lose our senses,
Men who stick at no offences
Will anon be here!
Piracy their dreadful trade is,
Pray you get you hence, young ladies,
While the coast is clear!

(FREDERIC and MABEL retire)

GIRLS   No, we must not lose our senses,
If they stick at no offences.
We should not be here!
Piracy their dreadful trade is,

GIRLS (Contd.)	Nice companions for young ladies! Let us disap- (*shriek*)

> (*During this chorus the* PIRATES *have entered stealthily, and formed in a semi-circle behind the* GIRLS. *As the* GIRLS *move to go off each* PIRATE *seizes a girl.* KING *seizes* EDITH *and* ISABEL, SAMUEL *seizes* KATE)

GIRLS	Too late!

PIRATES	Ha, ha!

GIRLS	Too late!

PIRATES	Ho, ho, Ha! ha! ha! ha! Ho, ho, ho, ho! Here's a first-rate opportunity To get married with impunity, And indulge in the felicity Of unbounded domesticity! You shall quickly be parsonified, Conjugally matrimonified, By a doctor of divinity, Who is located in this vicinity.

GIRLS	We have miss'd our opportunity Of escaping with impunity, So farewell to the felicity Of our maiden domesticity! We shall quickly be parsonified, Conjugally matrimonified, By a doctor of divinity, Who is located in this vicinity,

ALL	By a doctor of divinity, Who resides in this vicinity, By a doctor, a doctor, A doctor of divinity, Of divinity.

Music No. 12.	RECITATIVE (Mabel, Major-General, Samuel and Chorus) "Hold, Monsters!"

MABEL	(*Coming forward*) Hold, Monsters! Ere your pirate caravanserai Proceed, against our will, to wed us all, Just bear in mind that we are Wards in Chancery, And father is a Major-General!

SAMUEL	(*Cowed*) We'd better pause, or danger may befall; Their father is a Major-General!

GIRLS	Yes, yes, he is a Major-General!

> (*The* MAJOR-GENERAL *has entered unnoticed, on rock*)

15

GENERAL	Yes, yes, I am a Major-General!
SAMUEL	For he is a Major-General!
ALL	He is! Hurrah for the Major-General!
GENERAL	And it is, it is a glorious thing To be a Major-General!
ALL	It is! Hurrah for the Major-General Hurrah for the Major-General!

Music No. 13.   SONG (Major-General and Chorus)
"I Am the Very Model of a Modern Major-General"

GENERAL

I am the very model of a modern Major-General;
I've information vegetable, animal, and mineral;
I know the kings of England, and I quote the fights historical,
From Marathon to Waterloo, in order categorical;
I'm very well acquainted, too, with matters mathematical,
I understand equations, both the simple and quadratical,
About binomial Theorem I'm teeming with a lot of news,
With many cheerful facts about the square of the hypotenuse.

CHORUS

With many cheerful facts about the square of the hypotenuse,
With many cheerful facts about the square of the hypotenuse,
With many cheerful facts about the square of the hypotenpotenuse.

GENERAL

I'm very good at integral and differential calculus;
I know the scientific names of beings animalculous.
In short, in matters vegetable, animal, and mineral,
I am the very model of a modern Major-General.

CHORUS

In short, in matters vegetable, animal, and mineral,
He is the very model of a modern Major-General!

GENERAL

I know our mythic history, King Arthur's, and Sir Caradoc's,
I answer hard acrostics, I've a pretty taste for Paradox,
I quote, in Elegiacs, all the crimes of Heliogabalus!
In conics I can floor peculiarities parabolus.
I can tell undoubted Raphaels from Gerard Dows and Zoffanies.
I know the croaking chorus from the "Frogs" of Aristophanes!
Then I can hum a fugue of which I've heard the music's din afore,
And whistle all the airs from that infernal nonsense, "Pinafore!"

CHORUS

And whistle all the airs from that infernal nonsense, "Pinafore",
And whistle all the airs from that infernal nonsense, "Pinafore",
And whistle all the airs from that infernal nonsense, "Pina-pinafore".

GENERAL

Then I can write a washing bill in Babylonic cuneiform,
And tell you ev'ry detail of Caractacus's uniform.
In short, in matters vegetable, animal, and mineral,
I am the very model of a modern Major-General.

CHORUS	In short, in matters vegetable, animal, and mineral, He is the very model of a modern Major-General!
GENERAL	In fact, when I know what is meant by "mamelon" and "ravelin"; When I can tell at sight a Mauser rifle from a javelin; When such affairs as sorties and surprises I'm more wary at, And when I know precisely what is meant by commissariat; When I have learnt what progress has been made in modern gunnery; When I know more of tactics than a novice in a nunnery, In short, when I've a smattering of elemental strategy— You'll say a better Major-General has never *sat* a gee.
CHORUS	You'll say a better Major-General has never *sat* a gee, You'll say a better Major-General has never *sat* a gee, You'll say a better Major-General has never *sat* a, sat a gee.
GENERAL	For my military knowledge, tho' I'm plucky and adventury, Has only been brought down to the beginning of the century, But still, in matters vegetable, animal, and mineral, I am the very model of a modern Major-General.
CHORUS	But still, in matters vegetable, animal, and mineral, He is the very model of a modern Major-General.
GENERAL	And now that I've introduced myself I should like to have some idea of what's going on.
KATE	Oh, papa—we—
SAMUEL	Permit me, I'll explain in two words: we propose to marry your daughters.
GENERAL	Dear me!
GIRLS	Against our wills, papa—against our wills!
GENERAL	Oh, but you mustn't do that! May I ask—this is a picturesque uniform, but I'm not familiar with it. What are you?
KING	We are all single gentlemen.
GENERAL	Yes, I gathered that—anything else?
KING	No, nothing else.
EDITH	Papa, don't believe them; they are pirates—the famous Pirates of Penzance!
GENERAL	The Pirates of Penzance! I have often heard of them.
MABEL	All except this gentleman—(*indicating* FREDERIC)—who was a pirate once, but who is out of his indentures today, and who means to lead a blameless life evermore.
GENERAL	But wait a bit. I object to pirates as sons-in-law.

17

KING	We object to Major-Generals as fathers-in-law. But we waive that point. We do not press it. We look over it.
GENERAL	(*Aside*) Hah! an idea! (*Aloud*) And do you mean to say that you would deliberately rob me of these, the sole remaining props of my old age, and leave me to go through the remainder of my life unfriended, un-protected and alone?
KING	Well, yes, that's the idea.
GENERAL	Tell me, have you ever known what it is to be an orphan?
PIRATES	(*Disgusted*) Oh, dash it all!
KING	Here we are again!
GENERAL	I ask you, have you ever known what it is to be an orphan!
KING	Often!
GENERAL	Yes, orphan. Have you ever known what it is to be one?
KING	I say, often.
ALL	(*Disgusted*) Often, often, often.
GENERAL	I don't think we quite understand one another. I ask you, have you ever known what it is to be an orphan, and you say "orphan". As I understand you, you are merely repeating the word "orphan" to show that you understand me.
KING	I didn't repeat the word often.
GENERAL	Pardon me, you did indeed.
KING	I only repeated it once.
GENERAL	True, but you repeated it.
KING	But not often.
GENERAL	Stop: I think I see where we are getting confused. When you said "orphan", did you mean "orphan"—a person who has lost his parents, or "often"—frequently?
KING	Ah! I beg pardon—I see what you mean—frequently.
GENERAL	Ah! you said often—frequently.
KING	No, only once.
GENERAL	(*Irritated*) Exactly—you said often, frequently, only once.

Music No. 14.	FINALE—**ACT I** (Mabel, Kate, Edith, Ruth, Frederic, Samuel, King, Major-General and Chorus)

"Oh, Men of Dark and Dismal Fate"

GENERAL (*Recit.*) Oh, men of dark and dismal fate,
Forego your cruel employ,
Have pity on my lonely state,
I am an orphan boy!

SAM. & KING An orphan boy?
GENERAL An orphan boy!

SAM., KING & PIRATES How sad, an orphan boy!

GENERAL These children whom you see
Are all that I can call my own!

PIRATES Poor fellow!

GENERAL If pity you can feel,
Leave me my sole remaining joy—
See, at your feet they kneel:
Your hearts you cannot steel
Against the sad, sad tale of the lonely orphan boy!

PIRATES (*Sobbing*) Poor fellow!

SAM., KING & PIRATES See, at our feet they kneel!
Our hearts we cannot steel
Against the sad, sad tale of the lonely orphan boy!

SAMUEL The orphan boy!

SAM. & KING The orphan boy!
See, at our feet they kneel!
Our hearts we cannot steel
Against the tale of the lonely orphan boy.

PIRATES Poor fellow!

GENERAL (*Aside*) I'm telling a terrible story,
But it doesn't diminish my glory;
For they would have taken my daughters
Over the billowy waters,
If I hadn't, in elegant diction,
Indulged in an innocent fiction,
Which is not in the same category
As telling a regular terrible story.

MABEL, EDITH, KATE & GIRLS (*Aside*)
He is telling a terrible story
Which will tend to diminish his glory;
Though they would have taken his daughters

FRED., SAM., KING & PIRATES (*Aside*)
If he's telling a terrible story
He shall die by a death that is gory;
Yes, one of the cruellest slaughters

19

MABEL, EDITH, KATE & GIRLS (*Aside*) *contd.*		**FRED., SAM., KING & PIRATES** (*Aside*)
Over the billowy waters.		That ever were known in these waters.
It is easy, in elegant diction,		It is easy, in elegant diction,
To call it an innocent fiction,		To call it an innocent fiction,
But it comes in the same cate*gory*		But it comes in the same cate*gory*
As telling a regular terrible story.		As telling a regular terrible story.
It's easy, in elegant diction,	**& GEN.**	It's easy, in elegant diction,
To call it an innocent fiction,		To call it an innocent fiction,
But it comes in the same cate*gory*		But it comes in the same cate*gory*
As telling a regular story.		As telling a regular story.

KING

> Although our dark career
> Sometimes involves the crime of stealing,
> We rather think that we're
> Not altogether void of feeling.
> Although we live by strife,
> We're always sorry to begin it:
> For what, we ask, is life
> Without a touch of Poetry in it?

ALL

> (*Kneeling*) Hail Poetry, thou heav'n-born maid!
> Thou gildest e'en the Pirate's trade:
> Hail flowing fount of sentiment,
> All hail! all hail! Divine Emollient. (*All rise*)

KING

> (*Recit.*) You may go, for you're at liberty; our pirate rules protect you!
> And honorary members of our band we do elect you!

SAMUEL

> For he is an orphan boy!

ALL

> He is! Hurrah for the orphan boy!

GENERAL

> And it sometimes is a useful thing to be an orphan boy.

ALL

> It is! Hurrah for the orphan boy!
> Hurrah for the orphan boy!

MABEL, EDITH, KATE, FREDERIC & SAMUEL

> Oh, happy day, with joyous glee

& KING

> We
> They will away and married be!

CHORUS

> Oh, happy day, with joyous glee
> They will away and married be!

PRINCIPALS (less GEN.)

> Should it befall auspiciouslee,
>
> My
> Her sisters all will bridesmaids be!

CHORUS

> Should it befall auspiciouslee,
> Her sisters all will bridesmaids be!

ALL

> Oh, happy day, with joyous glee

ALL (Contd.)	We / They will away and married be. Should it befall auspiciouslee,
PRINCIPALS (less GEN.)	My / Her sisters all will bridesmaids be!
CHORUS and GENERAL	Should it befall auspiciouslee,
ALL	My / Her sisters all will bridesmaids be!

RUTH enters and comes down to FREDERIC

RUTH	(*Recit.*) Oh, master, ~~hear one word, I do implore you!~~ Remember Ruth, your Ruth, who kneels before you!
PIRATES	Yes, yes, remember Ruth, ~~who kneels before~~ you!
FREDERIC	Away, you did deceive me!
PIRATES	(*Threatening* RUTH) Away, you did deceive him!
RUTH	Oh, do not leave me!
PIRATES	Oh, do not leave her!
FREDERIC	Away, you grieve me!
PIRATES	Away, you grieve him!
FREDERIC	I wish you'd leave me!

(FREDERIC *casts* RUTH *from him*)

(*Exit* RUTH)

PIRATES	We wish you'd leave him!

FREDERIC, SAMUEL, KING, MAJOR-GENERAL & PIRATES
> Pray observe the magnanimity
> We display to lace and dimity!
> Never was such opportunity
> To get married with impunity!
> But we give up the felicity
> Of unbounded domesticity,
> Tho' a doctor of divinity
> Is located in this vicinity

MABEL, EDITH, KATE & GIRLS
> Pray observe the magnanimity
> They display to lace and dimity!
> Never was such opportunity
> To get married with impunity
> But they give up the felicity

21

MABEL, EDITH, KATE & GIRLS (Contd.)
        Of unbounded domesticity,
        Tho' a doctor of divinity,
        Is located in this vicinity.

ALL
        But   they/we   give up the felicity
        Of unbounded domesticity,
        But   they/we   give up the felicity
        Of unbounded domesticity,

EDITH, KATE & ALTOS	**SOPS. & MABEL**
Tho' a doctor of divinity,	Tho' a doc-
A doctor of divinity,	- - - tor, a
A doctor, a doctor of divinity	doctor, a doctor of divinity

ALL
        Tho' a doctor of divinity,
        Resides in this vicinity,
        Tho' a doctor, a doctor, resides in this vicinity,
        This vicinity.

> GIRLS *and* GENERAL *go up rocks, while* PIRATES *indulge in a wild dance of delight on stage. The* GENERAL *produces a British flag, and the* PIRATE KING *produces a black flag with skull and cross- bones. Enter* RUTH, *who makes a final appeal to* FREDERIC, *who casts her from him.*

END OF ACT I

ACT II

SCENE—*A Ruined Chapel by Moonlight. Ruined Gothic windows at back.* GENERAL STANLEY *discovered seated pensively, surrounded by his daughters.*

Music No. 1.   INTRODUCTION (Chorus of Girls) and SOLO (Mabel)
                     "Oh, Dry the Glist'ning Tear"

GIRLS
        Oh, dry the glist'ning tear
        That dews that martial cheek,
        Thy loving children hear,
        In them thy comfort seek.
        With sympathetic care
        Their arms around thee creep,
        For oh, they cannot bear
        To see their father weep!

                    (*Enter* MABEL)

MABEL
        Dear father, why leave your bed
        At this untimely hour,

MABEL (Contd.)	When happy daylight is dead, And darksome dangers lower? See, heav'n has lit her lamp, The twilight hour is past, And the chilly night air is damp, The dew is falling fast! Dear father, why leave your bed When happy daylight is dead?
GIRLS	Oh, dry the glist'ning tear That dews that martial cheek, Thy loving children hear, In them thy comfort seek. With sympathetic care Their arms around thee creep; For oh, they cannot bear To see their father weep!

FREDERIC *enters*

MABEL	Oh, Frederic, cannot you, in the calm excellence of your wisdom, reconcile it with your conscience to say something that will relieve my father's sorrow?
FREDERIC	I will try, dear Mabel. But why does he sit, night after night, in this draughty old ruin?
GENERAL	Why do I sit here? To escape from the pirates' clutches, I described myself as an orphan, and, heaven help me, I am no orphan! I come here to humble myself before the tombs of my ancestors, and to implore their pardon for having brought dishonour on the family escutcheon.
FREDERIC	But you forget, sir, you only bought the property a year ago, and the stucco in your baronial hall is scarcely dry.
GENERAL	Frederic, in this chapel are ancestors: you cannot deny that. With the estate, I bought the chapel and its contents. I don't know whose ancestors they *were*, but I know whose ancestors they *are*, and I shudder to think that their descendant by purchase (if I may so describe myself) should have brought disgrace upon what, I have no doubt, was an unstained escutcheon.
FREDERIC	Be comforted. Had you not acted as you did, these reckless men would assuredly have called in the nearest clergyman, and have married your large family on the spot.
GENERAL	I thank you for your proferred solace, but it is unavailing. I assure you, Frederic, that such is the anguish and remorse I feel at the abominable falsehood by which I escaped these easily deluded pirates, that I would go to their simple-minded chief this very night and confess all, did I not fear that the consequences would be most disastrous to myself. At what time does your expedition march against these scoundrels?

FREDERIC	At eleven, and before midnight I hope to have atoned for my involuntary association with the pestilent scourges by sweeping them from the face of the earth—and then, dear Mabel, you will be mine!
GENERAL	Are you devoted followers at hand?
FREDERIC	They are; they only wait my orders.

Music No. 2.   RECITATIVE (Frederic and Major-General)
"Then, Frederic, Let your Escort Lion-hearted"

GENERAL	Then, Frederic, let your escort lion-hearted Be summon'd to receive a gen'ral's blessing, Ere they depart upon their dread adventure.
FREDERIC	Dear sir, they come.

Enter POLICE, *marching in single file. They form in line, facing audience.*

Music No. 3.   CHORUS OF POLICE (with Solos: Mabel, Edith and Sergeant)
"When the Foeman Bares his Steel"

SERGEANT	When the foeman bares his steel,
CHORUS	Tarantara, tarantara!
SERGEANT	We uncomfortable feel!
CHORUS	Tarantara,
SERGEANT	And we find the wisest thing,
CHORUS	Tarantara, tarantara!
SERGEANT	Is to slap our chests and sing
CHORUS & SERGEANT	Tarantara!
SERGEANT	For when threaten'd with emeutes,
CHORUS	Tarantara, tarantara!
SERGEANT	And your heart is in your boots,
CHORUS	Tarantara!
SERGEANT	There is nothing brings it round, Like the trumpet's martial sound, Like the trumpet's martial sound,

SERGEANT	Ta-ran-ta-ra, ta-ran-ta- ra, ta-ran-ta-ra, ta-ran-ta- ra, ta-ran-ta-ra, ta-ran-ta-	**CHORUS**	Ta-ran-ta-ra, ta-ran-ta- ra, ra, ra, ra, ra, ra, ra, ra,

SERGEANT (Contd.)	ra, ta-ran-ta-ra, ta-ran-ta- ra, ta-ran-ta-ra, ta-ran-ta- ra, ta-ran-ta-ra, ta-ran-ta- ra, ta-ran-ta-ra, ta-ran-ta- ra, ra, ra, ta-ran-ta-ra!	CHORUS (Contd.)	ra, ra, ra, ra, ra, ra, ra, ra, ra, ra, ra, ra, ra, ra, ra, ta-ran-ta- ra, ra, ra, ta-ran-ta-ra!

MABEL
Go, ye heroes, go to glory,
Though ye die in combat gory,
Ye shall live in song and story.
Go to immortality!
Go to death, and go to slaughter;
Die, and ev'ry Cornish daughter
With her tears your grave shall water!
Go, ye heroes, go and die!

EDITH & KATE with GIRLS   Go, ye heroes, go and die!
Go, ye heroes, go and die!

SERGEANT   Tho' to us it's evident,

CHORUS   Tarantara, tarantara!

SERGEANT   These attentions are well meant,

CHORUS   Tarantara,

SERGEANT   Such expressions don't appear,

CHORUS   Tarantara, tarantara!

SERGEANT   Calculated men to cheer,

CHORUS   Tarantara,

SERGEANT   Who are going to meet their fate
In a highly nervous state,

CHORUS   Tarantara, tarantara, tarantara!

SERGEANT   Still to us it's evident
These attentions are well meant.

CHORUS   Tarantara, tarantara, tarantara,

EDITH   Go and do your best endeavour,
And before all links we sever,
We will say farewell for ever.
Go to glory and the grave!

GIRLS   Go to glory and the grave!
For your foes are fierce and ruthless,
False, unmerciful, and truthless,
Young and tender, old and toothless,
All in vain their mercy crave!

SERGEANT	We observe too great a stress
	On the risks that on us press,
	And of reference a lack
	To our chance of coming back;
	Still, perhaps it would be wise
	Not to carp or criticise,
	For it's very evident
	These attentions are well meant.

POLICE (Tenors)	Yes, it's very evident
(Basses)	These attentions are well meant,
(Tenors)	Evident,
(Basses)	Yes, well meant;
(Tenors)	Evident,

SERGEANT & ALL POLICE   Ah, yes, well meant!

MABEL & EDITH	GIRLS	SERGEANT & POLICE
		When the
Go, ye heroes,	Go, ye	foeman bares his steel, Ta-ran-ta-
go to glory!	heroes,	ra, ta-ran-ta-ra! We un-
Though ye die in combat	go to	comfortable feel, Ta-ran-ta-
gory,	glory!	ra! And we
Ye shall live in	Ye shall,	find the wisest thing, Ta-ran-ta-
song and story,	Ye shall	ra, ta-ran-ta-ra! Is to
Go to immortali-	live in	slap our chests and sing, Ta-ran-ta-
ty! Go to	story. Go to	ra! For when
death, and go to	death, and go to	threaten'd with emeutes, Ta-ran-ta-

MABEL	**EDITH with GIRLS**	
slaughter;	slaughter; Die, and	ra, ta-ran-ta-ra! And your
Die, and ev'ry Cornish	ev'ry Cornish	heart is in your boots, Ta-ran-ta-
daughter With her	daughter With her	ra! There is

MABEL, EDITH & GIRLS		
tears your grave shall		nothing brings it round Like the
water. Go, ye		trumpet's martial sound, Like the
heroes, go and		trumpet's martial
die! Go, ye		sound! Ta-ran-ta-ra, ta-ran-ta-

GIRLS	SERGEANT & TENORS	BASSES
heroes, go to	ra, Ta-ran-ta-ra, ta-ran-ta-	ra, ra, ra, ra,
immortality! Go ye	ra, ta-ran-ta-ra, ta-ran-ta-	ra, ra, ra, ra,
heroes, go to	ra, ta-ran-ta-ra, ta-ran-ta-	ra, ra, ra, ra,
immortality! Tho' ye	ra, ta-ran-ta-ra, ta-ran-ta-	ra, ra, ra, Ta-ran-ta-
die in combat gory, Ye shall	ra, ra, ra, ra,	ra, ra, ra, ra,
live in song and story; Go to	ra, ra, ra, Ta-ran-ta-	ra, ra, ra, Ta-ran-ta-
immortality!	ra, ta-ran-ta-ra, ta-ran-ta-ra!	ra, ta-ran-ta-ra, ta-ran-ta-ra!

GENERAL	Away, away!
POLICE	(*Without moving*) Yes, yes, we go!
GENERAL	These pirates slay!

POLICE	Tarantara!		
GENERAL	Then do not stay!		
POLICE	Tarantara!		
GENERAL	Then why this delay!		
POLICE	All right, we go!		
GIRLS	Yes, forward on the foe,	**POLICE**	Yes, forward on the foe! Yes, forward on the foe!
GENERAL	Yes, but you *don't* go!		
GIRLS	They go, they go! Yes, forward on the foe!	**POLICE**	We go, we go! Yes, forward on the foe! Yes, forward on the foe!
GENERAL	Yes, but you *don't* go!		
ALL BUT POLICE & GENERAL	At last they go! At last they go, at last they go! At last they really, really go!	**POLICE**	We go, we go! We go, we go! We go, we go, we go, we go!

(*Exeunt* POLICE)

(MABEL *tears herself from* FREDERIC *and exit, followed by her sisters, consoling her. The* GENERAL *and others follow.* FREDERIC *remains*)

Music No. 4.   RECITATIVE (Frederic) & TRIO (Ruth, Frederic and King)
"Now for the Pirates' Lair!"

FREDERIC   Now for the Pirates' lair! Oh, joy unbounded!
Oh, sweet relief! Oh, rapture unexampled
At last I may atone, in some slight measure,
For the repeated acts of theft and pillage,
Which, at a sense of duty's stern dictation,
I, circumstance's victim, have been guilty!

(KING *and* RUTH *appear at the window, armed*)

KING   Young Fred'ric! (*Covering him with pistol*)

FREDERIC   Who calls?

KING   Your late commander!

RUTH   And I, your little Ruth! (*Covering him with pistol*)

FREDERIC   Oh, mad intruders,
How dare ye face me?

FRED. (Contd.)   Know ye not, oh rash ones,
                         That I have doomed you to extermination?

                         (KING *and* RUTH *hold a pistol to each ear*)

KING   Have mercy on us; hear us, ere you slaughter.

FREDERIC   I do not think I ought to listen to you;
                         Yet, mercy should alloy our stern resentment,
                         And so, I will be merciful—say on!   *Have your say!*

Music No. 5.   TRIO (Ruth, Frederic and King)
                         "When you had Left our Pirate Fold"

RUTH   When you had left our pirate fold,
                         We tried to raise our spirits faint,
                         According to our custom old,
                         With quip and quibble quaint;
                         But all in vain, the quips we heard,
                         We lay and sobb'd upon the rocks,
                         Until to somebody occurr'd
                         A startling paradox.

FREDERIC   A paradox?

RUTH   A paradox,
                         A most ingenious paradox!
                         We've quips and quibbles heard in flocks,
                         But none to beat this paradox!

ALL THREE   A paradox, a paradox,
                         A most ingenious paradox.
                         Ha, ha, ha, ha, ha, ha, ha, ha,
                         This paradox!

KING   We knew your taste for curious quips.
                         For cranks and contradictions queer:
                         And with the laughter on our lips,
                         We wish'd you there to hear.
                         We said, "If we could tell it him,
                         How Fred'ric would the joke enjoy"
                         And so we've risk'd both life and limb
                         To tell it to our boy.

FREDERIC   (*Interested*) That paradox?

KING   (*Laughing*) That paradox,
                         That most ingenious paradox!
                         We've quips and quibbles heard in flocks,
                         But none to beat that paradox!

ALL THREE   A paradox, a paradox,
                         A most ingenious paradox.

ALL THREE (Contd.)	Ha, ha, ha, ha, ha, ha, ha, ha, That paradox!
KING	(*Recit.*) For some ridiculous reason, to which, however, I've no desire to be disloyal, Some person in authority—I don't know who—very likely the Astronomer Royal, Has decided that, although for such a beastly month as February, twenty-eight days as a rule are plenty: One year in every four his days shall be reckoned as nine-and-twenty. Through some singular coincidence—I shouldn't be surprised if it were owing to the agency of an ill-natured fairy, You are the victim of this clumsy arrangement, having been born in leap-year, on the twenty-ninth of February, And so, by a simple arithmetical process, you'll easily discover, That tho' you've lived twenty-one years, yet, if we go by birthdays, you're only five and a little bit over!
RUTH & KING	Ha, ha, ha, ha, ha, ha! Ho, ho, ho, ho!
FREDERIC	Dear me, Let's see! (*Counting on fingers*) Yes! yes! with yours my figures do agree!
RUTH & KING	Ha, ha, ha, ha, ha, ha, ha, ha!

(FREDERIC *more amused than any*)

FREDERIC	How quaint the ways of Paradox! At common sense she gaily mocks! Tho' counting in the usual way, Years twenty-one I've been alive, Yet, reck'ning by my natal day, Yet, reck'ning by my natal day, I am a little boy of five!
RUTH & KING	He is a little boy of five!
ALL	Ha, ha, ha, ha, ha, ha, ha, ha! A paradox, a paradox, A most ingenious paradox, Ha, ha, ha, ha, ha, ha, ha, ha! A paradox, Ha, ha, ha, ha, ha, ha, ha, ha! A curious paradox, Ha, ha, ha, ha, ha, ha, ha, ha! A most ingenious paradox.

(RUTH *and* KING *throw themselves back on seats, exhausted with laughter*)

FREDERIC	Upon my word, this is most curious—most absurdly whimsical. Five-and-a-quarter! No one would think it to look at me!

RUTH	You are glad now, I'll be bound, that you spared us. You would never have forgiven yourself when you discovered that you had killed *two of your comrades*.
FREDERIC	My comrades?
KING	(*Rises*) I'm afraid you don't appreciate the delicacy of your position. You were apprenticed to us—
FREDERIC	Until I reached my twenty-first year.
KING	No, until you reached your twenty-first *birthday* (producing document), and, going by birthdays, you are as yet only five-and-a-quarter.
FREDERIC	You don't mean to say you are going to hold me to that?
KING	No, we merely remind you of the fact, and leave the rest to your sense of duty.
RUTH	(*Rises*) Your sense of duty!
FREDERIC	(*Wildly*) Don't put it on that footing! As I was merciful to you just now, be merciful to me! I implore you not to insist on the letter of your bond just as the cup of happiness is at my lips!
RUTH	We insist on nothing; we content ourselves with pointing out to you *your duty*.
KING	Your duty!
FREDERIC	(*After a pause*) Well, you have appealed to my sense of duty, and my duty is only too clear. I abhor your infamous calling; I shudder at the thought that I have ever been mixed up with it; but duty is before all—at any price I will do my duty.
KING	Bravely spoken! Come, you are one of us once more.
FREDERIC	Lead on, I follow. (*Suddenly*) Oh, horror!
KING & RUTH	What is the matter?
FREDERIC	Ought I to tell you? No, no, I cannot do it; and yet, as one of your band—
KING	Speak out, I charge you by that sense of conscientiousness to which we have never yet appealed in vain.
FREDERIC	General Stanley, the father of my Mabel—
KING & RUTH	Yes, yes!
FREDERIC	He escaped from you on the plea that he was an orphan!
KING	He did!

FREDERIC	It breaks my heart to betray the honoured father of the girl I adore, but as your apprentice I have no alternative. It is my duty to tell you that General Stanley is no orphan!
KING & RUTH	What!
FREDERIC	More than that, he never was one!
KING	Am I to understand that, to save his contemptible life, he dared to practise on our credulous simplicity? (FREDERIC *nods as he weeps.*) Our revenge shall be swift and terrible. We will go and collect our band and attack Tremorden Castle this very night.
FREDERIC	But—stay—
KING	Not a word! He is doomed! *Pause!*
Music No. 6.	TRIO (Ruth, Frederic and King) "Away, Away! My Heart's on Fire!"
KING & RUTH	Away, away! my heart's on fire! I burn this base deception to repay. This very night my vengeance dire Shall glut itself in gore. Away, away!
FREDERIC	Away, away! ere I expire— I find my duty hard to do today! My heart is filled with anguish dire; It strikes me to the core! Away, away!
KING	With falsehood foul He trick'd us of our brides; Let vengeance howl; The Pirate so decides. Our nature stern He softened with his lies! And, in return, Tonight the traitor dies.
RUTH & FRED.	Yes, yes! tonight the traitor dies!
ALL	Yes, yes! tonight the traitor dies!
RUTH	Tonight he dies!
KING	Yes, or early tomorrow.
FREDERIC	His girls likewise?
RUTH	They will welter in sorrow.

KING	The one soft spot
RUTH	In their natures they cherish—
FREDERIC	And all who plot
KING	To abuse it shall perish!
ALL THREE	Tonight he dies! Yes, or early tomorrow. His girls likewise, they will welter in sorrow; The one soft spot In their natures they cherish, And all who plot To abuse it shall perish! Away, away, away! Tonight the traitor dies! Away, away! tonight, tonight, Tonight the traitor dies! Tonight! Away!

Exeunt KING *and* RUTH

Enter MABEL

Music No. 7.	RECITATIVE & DUET (Mabel and Frederic) "All is Prepar'd, Your Gallant Crew Await You!"
MABEL	All is prepar'd, your gallant crew await you. My Frederic in tears! It cannot be That lion-heart quails at the coming conflict?
FREDERIC	No, Mabel, no. A terrible disclosure Has just been made! Mabel, my dearly-lov'd one, I bound myself to serve the Pirate Captain Until I reach'd my one and twentieth birthday!
MABEL	But you *are* twenty-one?
FREDERIC	I've just discover'd That I was born in leap-year, and that birthday Will not be reach'd by me till nineteen forty!
MABEL	Oh, horrible! catastrophe appalling!
FREDERIC	And so, farewell!
MABEL	No, no! Ah, Fred'ric, hear me!
Music No. 8.	DUET (Mabel and Frederic) "Stay, Fred'ric, Stay!"
MABEL	Stay, Fred'ric, stay! They have no legal claim,

MABEL (Contd.)	No shadow of a shame Will fall upon thy name; Stay, Fred'ric, stay!
FREDERIC	Nay, Mabel, nay! Tonight I quit these walls, The thought my soul appals; But when stern Duty calls, I must obey!
MABEL	Stay, Fred'ric, stay!
FREDERIC	Nay, Mabel, nay;
MABEL	They have no claim—
FREDERIC	But duty's name.

FREDERIC	The thought my soul appals; But when stern duty calls,	**MABEL**	No shadow of a shame Will fall upon thy name;

MABEL	Stay, Fred'ric, stay!
FREDERIC	I must obey!
MABEL	Ah, leave me not to pine Alone and desolate; No fate seem'd fair as mine, No happiness so great! And nature, day by day, Has sung, in accents clear, This joyous roundelay; "He loves thee—he is here. Fal-la, la, la, Fal-la, la, la! He loves thee—he is here. Fal-la, la, la, Fal-la!"
FREDERIC	Ah, must I leave thee here In endless night to dream, Where joy is dark and drear, And sorrow all supreme! Where nature, day by day, Will sing, in altered tone, This weary roundelay: "He loves thee—he is gone. Fal-la, la, la, Fal-la, la, la! He loves thee—he is gone.
BOTH	Fal-la, la, la, Fal-la!
FREDERIC	(*Recit.*) In 1940 I of age shall be; I'll then return, and claim you, I declare it!
MABEL	It seems so long!

33

FREDERIC	Swear that, till then, you will be true to me!
MABEL	Yes, I'll be strong! By all the Stanleys, dead and gone, I swear it!
BOTH	Oh, here is love, and here is truth, And here is food for joyous laughter; He / She will be faithful to his / her sooth, Till we are wed, and even after!
FREDERIC	Oh, here is love, and here is truth,
MABEL	Oh, here is love, and here is truth,

MABEL	**FREDERIC**	She will be faithful to
He will be faithful to his sooth,		her sooth, Till we are wed, and even after,

FREDERIC	Till we are wed, and even after,
MABEL	Till we are wed,
FREDERIC	And even after!
MABEL	Yes, even after!
BOTH	Oh, here is love, and here is truth, And here is food for joyous laughter; He / She will be faithful to his / her sooth,
MABEL	Till we are wed, and even after!
BOTH	He / She will be faithful to his / her sooth,
FREDERIC	Till we are wed and
BOTH	and / even after, even after! Oh, here is love, and here is truth, Oh, here is love, is love!

FREDERIC *rushes to window and leaps out*

Music No. 9.	RECITATIVE (Mabel) and Chorus of Police "No, I'll Be Brave"
MABEL	(*Almost fainting*) No, I'll be brave! Oh, family descent, How great thy charm, thy sway how excellent! Come, one and all, undaunted men in blue, A crisis, now; affairs are coming to!

34

Enter POLICE, *marching in single file*

SERGEANT   Tho' in body and in mind,

CHORUS   Tarantara, tarantara!

SERGEANT   We are timidly inclined,

CHORUS   Tarantara!

SERGEANT   And anything but blind,

CHORUS   Tarantara, tarantara!

SERGEANT   To the danger that's behind,

CHORUS   Tarantara!

SERGEANT   Yet, when the danger's near,

CHORUS   Tarantara, tarantara!

SERGEANT   We manage to appear,

CHORUS   Tarantara!

SERGEANT   As insensible to fear
       As anybody here, as anybody

SERGEANT	CHORUS
here. Ta-ran-ta- ra, ta-ran-ta-ra, ta-ran-ta- ra, ta-ran-ta-ra, ta-ran-ta- ra, ta-ran-ta-ra, ta-ran-ta- ra, ta-ran-ta-ra, ta-ran-ta- ra, ta-ran-ta-ra, ta-ran-ta- ra, ta-ran-ta-ra, ta-ran-ta- ra, ra, ra, ta-ran-ta-ra!	Ta-ran-ta-ra, ta-ran-ta- ra, ra, ra, ra, ra, ra, ra, ra, ra, ra, ra, ra, ra, ra, ra, ra, ra, ra, ra, ra, ra, ra, ra, ta-ran-ta- ra, ra, ra, ta-ran-ta-ra!

MABEL   (*Spoken*) Sergeant, approach! Young Frederic was to have led you to death and glory.

ALL   (*Chanted*) That is not a pleasant way of putting it.

MABEL   (*Spoken*) No matter; he will not so lead you, for he has allied himself once more with his old associates.

ALL   (*Chanted*) He has acted shamefully!

MABEL   (*Spoken*) You speak falsely. You know nothing about it. He has acted nobly.

ALL   (*Chanted*) He has acted nobly!

MABEL	(*Spoken*) Dearly as I loved him before, his heroic sacrifice to his sense of duty has endeared him to me tenfold. He has done his duty. I will do mine. Go ye and do yours.

Exit MABEL

ALL	(*Chanted*) Right oh!
SERGEANT	(*Spoken*) This is perplexing.
ALL	(*Chanted*) We cannot understand it at all.
SERGEANT	(*Spoken*) Still, as he is actuated by a sense of duty—
ALL	(*Chanted*) That makes a difference, of course. At the same time we repeat, we cannot understand it at all.
SERGEANT	(*Spoken*) No matter; our course is clear. We must do our best to capture these pirates alone. It is most distressing to us to be the agents whereby our erring fellow-creatures are deprived of that liberty which is so dear to all—but we should have thought of that before we joined the force.
ALL	(*Chanted*) We should!
SERGEANT	(*Spoken*) It is too late now!
ALL	(*Chanted*) It is!

Music No. 10.   SONG (Sergeant and Chorus of Police)
"When a Felon's not Engaged in his Employment"

SERGEANT	When a felon's not engaged in his employment—
CHORUS	his employment,
SERGEANT	Or maturing his felonious little plans—
CHORUS	little plans,
SERGEANT	His capacity for innocent enjoyment—
CHORUS	-cent enjoyment,
SERGEANT	Is just as great as any honest man's—
CHORUS	honest man's.
SERGEANT	Our feeling we with difficulty smother—
CHORUS	-culty smother,
SERGEANT	When constabulary duty's to be done,—

CHORUS	to be done.
SERGEANT	Ah, take one consideration with another—
CHORUS	with another,
SERGEANT	A policeman's lot is not a happy one.
CHORUS **plus SERGEANT**	Ah, When constabulary duty's to be done,— to be done, A policeman's lot is not a happy one,— happy one.
SERGEANT	When the enterprising burglar's not a-burgling—
CHORUS	not a-burgling,
SERGEANT	When the cut-throat isn't occupied in crime—
CHORUS	-pied in crime,
SERGEANT	He loves to hear the little brook a-gurgling—
CHORUS	brook a-gurgling,
SERGEANT	And listen to the merry village chime—
CHORUS	village chime.
SERGEANT	When the coster's finished jumping on his mother—
CHORUS	on his mother,
SERGEANT	He loves to lie a-basking in the sun,—
CHORUS	in the sun.
SERGEANT	Ah, take one consideration with another—
CHORUS	with another,
SERGEANT	A policeman's lot is not a happy one.
CHORUS **plus SERGEANT**	Ah, When constabulary duty's to be done,— to be done, A policeman's lot is not a happy one,— happy one.
Music No. 11.	SOLO (Sergeant) and Chorus of Pirates and Police "A Rollicking Band of Pirates We"

37

PIRATES	(*Off stage*) A rollicking band of Pirates we,
	Who, tired of tossing on the sea,
	Are trying their hand at a burglaree,
	With weapons grim and gory.
SERGEANT	Hush, hush, I hear them on the manor poaching;
	With stealthy steps the Pirates are approaching!
PIRATES	We are not coming for plate or gold;
	A story General Stanley told;
	We seek penalty fifty-fold,
	For General Stanley's story!
POLICE	They seek a penalty
PIRATES	Fifty-fold!
	We seek a penalty
POLICE	Fifty-fold!
ALL	We They seek a penalty fifty-fold,
	For General Stanley's story!
SERGEANT	They come in force, with stealthy stride;
	Our obvious course is now—to hide!
POLICE	Tarantara, tarantara! etc.

> (POLICE *conceal themselves. As they do so, the* PIRATES *are seen appearing at ruined windows. They enter cautiously, and come down stage.* SAMUEL *is laden with burglarious tools and pistols, etc.*)

Music No. 12.   CHORUS of Pirates, with SOLO (Samuel)
"With Cat-like Tread"

PIRATES	(*Very loud*) With cat-like tread,
	Upon our prey we steal;
	In silence dread
	Our cautious way we feel!
	No sound at all,
	We never speak a word;
	A fly's foot-fall
	Would be distinctly heard—
POLICE	(*Pianissimo*) Tarantara, tarantara!—
PIRATES	So stealthily the Pirate creeps,
	While all the household soundly sleeps.

PIRATES		**POLICE**	
Come,		Ra, ra,	
friends,		ra, ra,	
who			
plough the		ra, ra,	

PIRATES (Contd.)		POLICE (Contd.)	
	sea,		ra, ra,
	Truce to		ra,
	navi—		ra,
	gation,		ra, ra,
	Take an—		ra,
	other		ra,
	station,		ra, ra,
	Let's		ra, ra,
	va-		ra, ra,
	ry		
	pira-		ra, ra,
	cee		ra, ra,
	With a		ra,
	little		ra,
	burglaree!		ra, ra, ra!
	Come		Ra, ra,
	friends,		ra, ra,
	who		
	plough the		ra, ra,
	sea,		ra, ra,
	Truce to		ra,
	navi-		ra,
	gation,		ra, ra,
	Take an-		ra,
	other		ra,
	station;		ra, ra,
	Let's		ra, ra,
	va-		ra, ra,
	ry		
	pira-		ra, ra,
	cee,		ra, ra,
	With a little burglaree!		ra, Ta-ran-ta-ra, ra, ra!

SAMUEL   (*Distributing implements to various members of the gang*)
Here's your crowbar, and your centrebit,
Your life preserver you may want to hit!
Your silent matches, your dark lantern seize!
Take your file and your skeletonic keys!

Enter KING, FREDERIC *and* RUTH

POLICE   Tarantara,

PIRATES   With cat-like tread,

POLICE   Tarantara-

PIRATES (*fortissimo*)		POLICE	
	In silence dread,		ra!
	With cat-like tread,		
	Upon our prey we steal,		
	In silence dread		
	Our cautious way we feel!		
	No sound at all,		

39

PIRATES (contd.)	We never speak a word; A fly's foot-fall Would be distinctly heard!		

PIRATES		POLICE	Ta-ran-ta-
	Come,	(*pianissimo*)	ra, ra,
	friends,		ra, ra,
	who		
	plough the		ra, ra,
	sea,		ra, ra,
	Truce to		ra,
	navi-		ra,
	gation,		ra, ra,
	Take an-		ra,
	other		ra,
	station;		ra, ra,
	Let's		ra, ra,
	va-		ra, ra,
	ry		
	pira-		ra, ra,
	cee		ra, ra,
	With a little burglaree!		ra. Ta-ran-ta-ra, ra, ra,
	With cat-like tread		ta-ran-ta-ra,
	Upon our prey we steal;		Ta-ran-ta-ra, ra, ra,
	In silence dread		Ta-ran-ta-ra,
	Our cautious way we feel.		ta-ran-ta-ra, ra, ra!

Music No. 13.	RECITATIVE (Frederic, King, Major-General, Police and Pirates) "Hush, Hush, Not a Word!"

FREDERIC	Hush, hush! not a word; I see a light inside! The Major-Gen'ral comes, so quickly hide!

PIRATES	Yes, yes, the Major-Gen'ral comes!

(PIRATES *conceal themselves*)

Exeunt KING, FREDERIC, SAMUEL *and* RUTH

POLICE	Yes, yes, the Major-Gen'ral comes!

GENERAL	(*Entering in dressing-gown, carrying a light*) Yes, yes, the Major-Gen'ral comes! Tormented with the anguish dread Of falsehood unaton'd, I lay upon my sleepless bed, And toss'd, and turn'd, and groan'd; The man who finds his conscience ache No peace at all enjoys: And as I lay in bed awake, I thought I heard a noise.

PIRATES & POLICE	He thought he heard a noise; Ha, ha!

GENERAL	No, all is still, In dale, on hill, My mind is set at ease; So still the scene, It must have been The sighing of the breeze.
Music No. 14.	SONG (Major-General and Chorus of Pirates and Police) and FINALE "Sighing Softly to the River"
GENERAL	Sighing softly to the river, Comes the loving breeze; Setting nature all a-quiver, Rustling thro' the trees—
CHORUS	Thro' the trees.
GENERAL	And the brook, in rippling measure, Laughs for very love, While the poplars, in their pleasure, Wave their arms above.
CHORUS	Yes, the trees for very love, Wave their leafy arms above.
ALL	River, river, little river, May thy loving prosper e'er; Heaven speed thee, poplar tree, May thy wooing happy be, Heaven speed thee, poplar tree, May thy wooing happy be!
GENERAL	Yet, the breeze is but a rover; When he wings away! Brook and poplar mourn a lover! Sighing, "Well-a-day!"
CHORUS	"Well-a-day!"
GENERAL	Ah, the doing and undoing That the rogue could tell; When the breeze is out a-wooing, Who can woo so well?
CHORUS	Shocking tales the rogue could tell, Nobody can woo so well.
ALL	Pretty brook thy dream is over, For thy love is but a rover; Sad the lot of poplar trees, Courted by a fickle breeze, Sad the lot of poplar trees, Courted by a fickle breeze!

	(*Enters the* GENERAL's *daughters, led by* MABEL, *all in white peignoires and nightcaps, and carrying lighted candles.*)
GIRLS	Now what is this, and what is that, and why does father leave his rest At such a time of night as this, so very incompletely dress'd? Dear father is, and always was, the most methodical of men; It's his invariable rule to go to bed at half-past ten. What strange occurrence can it be that calls dear father from his rest At such a time of night as this, so very incompletely dress'd! So very incompletely dress'd, At such a time of night.
	Enter KING, SAMUEL *and* FREDERIC
KING	(*Spoken*) Forward, my men, and seize that General there!
	(*They seize the* GENERAL)
GIRLS	(*Sung*) The pirates! the pirates! oh, despair!
PIRATES	(*Springing up*) Yes, we're the pirates; so despair!
GENERAL	Frederic here! Oh joy! Oh rapture! Summon your men, and effect their capture!
MABEL	Frederic, save us!
FREDERIC	Beautiful Mabel, I would if I could, but I am not able.
PIRATES	He's telling the truth, he is not able.
KING	With base deceit You worked upon our feelings; Revenge is sweet, And flavours all our dealings! With courage rare And resolution manly, For death prepare, Unhappy Gen'ral Stanley!
MABEL	(*Wildly*) Is he to die, unshriven, unanneal'd?
GIRLS	Oh, spare him!
MABEL	Will no one in his cause a weapon wield?
GIRLS	Oh, spare him!
POLICE	(*Springing up*) Yes, we are here, though hitherto conceal'd!
GIRLS	Oh, rapture!

POLICE	So to Constabulary, pirates yield!
GIRLS	Oh, rapture!

(*A struggle ensues between* PIRATES *and* POLICE. *Eventually the* POLICE *are overcome, and fall prostrate, the* PIRATES *standing over them with drawn swords*)

CHORUS OF POLICE & PIRATES

You
We triumph now, for well we trow

Our
Your mortal career's cut short;

No pirate band will take its stand
At the Central Criminal Court!

SERGEANT	To gain a brief advantage you've contrived; But your proud triumph will not be long-lived.
KING	Don't say you're orphans, for we know that game!
SERGEANT	On your allegiance we've a stronger claim; We charge you yield, we charge you yield In Queen Victoria's name!
KING	(*Baffled*) You do?
POLICE	We do! We charge you yield, in Queen Victoria's name!

(PIRATES *kneel.* POLICE *stand over them triumphantly*)

KING	We yield at once, with humbled mien, Because, with all our faults, we love our Queen!
POLICE	Yes, yes, with all their faults, they love their Queen!
ALL	Yes, yes, with all their/our faults, they/we love their/our Queen!

(POLICE, *holding* PIRATES *by the collar, take out hand-kerchiefs and weep*)

GENERAL	Away with them, and place them at the bar!

Enter RUTH

RUTH	One moment, let me tell you who they are: They are no members of the common throng, They are all noblemen, who have gone wrong.
GIRLS	They are all noblemen, who have gone wrong.

GENERAL   No Englishman unmov'd that statement hears!
Because, with all our faults, we love our House of Peers:
I pray you pardon me, ex-Pirate King!
Peers will be Peers, and youth will have its fling!
Resume your ranks, and legislative duties,
And take my daughters, all of whom are beauties!

FINALE

MABEL   Poor wand'ring ones,
Though ye have surely strayed,
Take heart of grace,
Your steps retrace,
Poor wand'ring ones!
Poor wand'ring ones,
If such poor love as ours
Can help you find true peace of mind,
Why, take it, it is

MABEL	EDITH	KATE	FRED., KING & SAM	CHORUS
yours				Poor wand'ring
	Poor	Poor	Poor	one,
Ah, ah, -				
- - - ah,	wan-	wan-	wan-	
ah,	d'ring	d'ring	d'ring	
ah,	one,	one,	one,	Poor wond'ring
	Poor	Poor	Poor	one,
Ah, ah, -				
- - - ah,	wan-	wan-	wan-	
ah,	d'ring	d'ring	d'ring	
ah!	one,	one,	one,	

MABEL & EDITH		KATE, FRED., KING, SAM & CHORUS		
	Fair days will		Take	
	shine.		heart,	
	Take		take	
	heart, - -		heart,	
	- - - -			
			Take	
	take		any	
	mine!		heart,	
	Take		take	
	heart! - -		ours!	
	- - - -			
			Take heart,	
	- - - -			
			take ours!	
	- - - -			
	Take			
	mine!		Take	

(MABEL and KATE *tacet*)

EDITH		ALL OTHERS	heart, Fair days will shine,
	Take		Take
	heart,		heart,
	Fair days will		Fair days will
	shine,		shine,

ALL   Take heart,
            Take heart,
            Take heart,
            Take ours!

CURTAIN

Printed and bound in Great Britain

12' 3" + 5'

15'